Sketches of India

with

Forty Photographic

Illustrations

Joan V. Bondurant

IMAGO
PRESS
TUCSON ARIZONA

Published in the United States of America by:

Imago Press
3710 East Edison
Tucson AZ 85716

Library of Congress Cataloging-in-Publication Data

Bondurant, Joan V. (Joan Valérie), 1918-
Sketches of India : with forty photographic illustrations / Joan V. Bondurant.—1st ed.
p. cm.
Previous ed.: Ann Arbor, Mich. : Craft Press, 1946.
ISBN-13: 978-0-9725303-4-7 (pbk. : alk. paper)
ISBN-10: 0-9725303-4-7 (pbk. : alk. paper)
1. India—Description and travel. 2. India—Social life and customs. I. Title.

DS413.B668 2005
915.4—dc22
2005017843

First Edition published by Imago Press in 2005

Cover Design and Book Design: Leila Joiner
Text set in Minion Pro

ISBN 0-9725303-4-7
ISBN 978-0-9725303-4-7

Printed in the United States of America on Acid-Free Paper

Dedicated to

Mother and Dad

Foreword

In these nine brief sketches, I have tried to record a few of my impressions of life in India as I saw and lived it during my near two years' sojourn in that great land.

To treat adequately any part of the complexities which characterize the Indian scene is a matter for more serious writing. I have intended, here, simply to put into words a few of my surface glimpses of India.

If this booklet in any measure satisfies the desire of those good friends who have urged me to write it and so share with them my pictures and notes, then I shall be pleased with having made the effort.

—Joan V. Bondurant

Author's Note

The Hindī and Urdū words occurring in the text of these sketches have been transliterated from the original scripts to English spellings as accurately as simplicity will allow. The exact pronunciations cannot adequately be indicated by the simple use of the Roman alphabet. However, if the vowels of the italicized words are pronounced as in Italian—with the exception of *a* which should be pronounced as the *u* in *but*, and *i* which should be pronounced as the *i* in *pin*—a close approximation to the correct pronunciation will result.

a as the *u* in *but*	*e* as the *e* in *they*
ā as the *a* in *father*	*o* as the *o* in *old*
i as the *i* in *pin*	*u* as the *oo* in *foot*
ī as the *i* in *machine*	*ū* as the *oo* in *boot*

With regard to the consonants, it is sufficient here to note that *q* should be pronounced as *k* and *th* as the *th* combination in *hothouse.*

Since the system of transliteration from Hindī and Urdū has not been popularly standardized, there is considerable variance in the English spelling of Hindī and Urdū words. I have tried, in this text, to adhere as strictly as possible to the above system, which I believe to be the most nearly accurate of the simpler systems. In the case of certain words that have become a part of the English language, e.g., *curry* (*kari*), *coolie* (*quli*), and *jungle* (*jangal*), I have given the popular English spellings and have not italicized the words. In the case of proper nouns, the romanized spelling is based upon the most common usage in India; the reader will note *Muslim* instead of *Moslem* and *Mathurā* instead of *Muttra.*

J. V. B.

The Sketches

- Delhi, old and new: India's Imperial Capital
- Servants
- Udaipur, the Heart of Rājputānā
- Modes of Dress
- Āgra, City of the Tāj Mahal
- Animals
- Ajmer and Pushkar, King of Sacred Sites
- Food and Famine
- Rishikesh on the Sacred Ganges

Prologue

How does a young graduate from the University of Michigan with two Bachelor Degrees find herself in India translating Japanese documents?

The answer is Joan V. Bondurant's unrelenting desire to serve her country in time of war. World War II broke out while Joan was completing her studies in Music in 1943. She quickly determined to find a way to serve her country in any way possible. Unable to pass U.S. Military health requirements, she noted that two schools in America were preparing students to translate the Japanese ideographs. Although the University of Michigan was one of the schools with this specialized training, the program was open only to men, but Joan Bondurant would not be deterred by this regulation.

Having an innate sense of power, Joan decided to sit at the door to the Japanese Language Class until she gained admission. That action worked, and she was admitted to the program, which eventually prepared her to accept work at the Office of Strategic Service (OSS) in San Francisco after graduation.

One day, after many weeks of training at the OSS, Joan was sent for by her employer and asked if she would accept assignment to India. She was given fifteen minutes to answer the question. With little or no hesitation, she took the job and was sent to Washington for further training along with an assistant, Maureen Patterson. They soon found themselves on a troop ship with a few military nurses, bound for what they knew was India, but they were unable to reveal to the nurses their destination: Bombay.

While in India, Bondurant and Patterson were stationed at the New Delhi Office, where they worked eliciting meaning from

Japanese ideographs. Because Joan and Maureen each learned half of the Japanese ideographs, together they were able to eke out the meaning of intercepted letters, maps, directives, and orders. They served in this capacity for two years before retiring to the United States.

After World War II, Joan returned to Great Bend, Kansas in 1946, where she first published *Sketches of India*. This newly-revised edition of the book allows the reader to see through her eyes the place sometimes referred to as "the most foreign of all countries"—India.

Joan returned to India several times, immersing herself in this wondrous country, searching out Indian friends, and soon becoming "the fourth daughter" of an Indian family, the Uttam Singhs, who treated her as one of their own. This experience adds depth to her descriptions, as does the inclusion of her poetry, written while she was in India.

Readers can look through the eyes of an American woman in India at a momentous time in India's history. Enjoy this vicarious trip!

Edna Cardish, Editor

Delhi, Old and New:
India's Imperial Capital

The author on top of Himayun's tomb, New Delhi

"If there be paradise on earth, this is it, this is it, this is it."

I stepped out of an air-conditioned train compartment into the hottest New Delhi day of 1944. A two years' stay in India's Imperial Capital was to teach me how to take the successive days of shade-read temperatures soaring above 110 degrees and the fireless winter nights of near-freezing breezes. The constant attendance of servants, the pleasurable distractions of foreign, friendly people, the glories of discovering ancient and modern civilizations of which a Westerner scarcely dreams—these parts of life in India dimmed the notability of an "impossible" climate.

My first visit to Chāndi Chauk, the famous "silver street" of Delhi, left me with impressions chiefly of horror and confusion. Squalor, din and disorder of seeming millions of people, misplaced cows, odd dogs and funeral processions rewarded the superficial glance. An advertisement plugging the latest drug for "sure conception" seemed somehow remarkable in this land of endless bearing and dying of children. And the "Chauk" appeared less a market than essential melee.

As I began to look a little deeper, and as I became less a stranger in India, I came to appreciate the attitude which tolerates seeming disorder, and I came to delight in the beauty of variety and the variety of beauty in multitudinous costumes. The fuschia red of a Marātha turban, the full-blown cut of the Panjābi *pājāmā*, the black-tasseled fez of a Muslim shopkeeper—these costumes provided the suggestion of a wealth and variety of cultures. The clatter of *tangā*-pony hoofs, the bells of the rickshaw pullers, an occasional melody from an Indian flute, and the seeming Babel to the ignorant ear of many languages indicated the challenging diversity on all levels of Indian life. Months in India brought me an understanding that seeming inefficiency of all physical life indicated something quite above ineffectiveness of pursuit and effort. I came at length to glimpse a bit of the spirit which marks the unity of India—and one of its facets is the immense relevance of an "eternal now."

As life ambles on in Chāndi Chauk, the great Jāmi Masjid towers up from the bazaars, commanding a view which sweeps the breadth of old and New Delhi. This impressive mosque of great Moghul architecture is built in all the tradition of Eastern grandeur. Of red sandstone, the mosque has three large domes of marble with inset black strips. Its two mammoth minarets have remarkable flights of stone steps leading to their summits. The Jāmi Masjid is said to be the second largest mosque in the world, and it is the most revered Muslim structure in the whole of India.

A short distance from Jāmi Masjid stands the massive Red Fort situated on the right bank of the Jamnā river. Built of red sandstone, the Fort's mighty walls surmounted with frequent towers extend a mile and a half in circumference. Within the great walls are found rare gems of buildings where justice and the business of the great Moghul empires transpired in feudal splendor. Semitropical gardens fill in the distances between buildings.

The Dīwān-i-Ām, Hall of Public Audience, within the Fort, is a large hall lavishly gilded and enclosed by arcaded cloisters. This structure is outdone in beauty by the magnificent Dīwān-i-Khās, Hall of Private Audience. A pavilion of white marble, this building boasts elaborately carved pillars inlaid with precious gems in delicately turned floral designs. Down the length of the pavilion through Moghul archways, the famous Persian couplet in gold and brilliant-colored inlay is inscribed above a scales of justice: "If there be paradise on earth, this is it, this is it, this is it."

From the Dīwān-i-Khās, looking through a marbled portico, the finest gem within the whole of the fort structure charms the visitor's view. The Motī Masjid or Pearl Mosque is built of

On Chāndi Chauk, India's "Silver Street"

The Qutb Minār, an architectural wonder-of-the-world

dazzling white marble with a courtyard enclosed by red sandstone walls. Here are the inevitable minarets, delicate in structure, the four smooth pillars, and paintings of rare quality overhead on poised arches.

The Red Fort is another of the glories in construction conceived by the great Moghul, Shāh Jahān, builder of the Tāj Mahal. It has stood for over three centuries, testament to the one-time glory of the great Moghuls.

Stretching away from old Delhi lies the present well-planned Imperial Capital of India. New Delhi, the seventh historical city bearing the name "Delhi," was proclaimed Imperial Capital of British India on 12 December, 1911. The historic myth that, whenever the seat of government in India is placed at Delhi, the political regime in India subsequently comes to a rapid decline is delightfully repeated by Indians today. Certainly, Delhi has a wealth of historical memories, and the outlying territory, especially to the south of New Delhi, is dotted with extensive remains of forts and cities and monuments.

On the outskirts of the newest Delhi stands Emperor Humayun's tomb. Surrounded by a magnificent garden and screened by high walls through which one may pass by superb gateways to the west and south, this tomb displays its huge marble dome for miles around. The tomb is flanked by a long massive rampart. On each corner towers a red sandstone minaret with patchwork of exquisite marble. The fountains and delightful ponds in the garden of the tomb add a natural flavor to this great historic monument.

The environs of Delhi boast an architectural wonder of the world. The Qutb Minār, rising to a height of 238 feet, is the highest single tower in the world. Built of red sandstone, the Minār's base is 47 feet, and its summit is nine feet in diameter. It is believed by some authorities to have been built by Qutb-ud-dīn Aibak as a tower of victory; others hold that it is a normal minaret; and others believe the Qutb Minār to have been built by

The white marble Motī Masjid (Pearl Mosque), Red Fort, Delhi

"If there be Paradise on Earth, this is it, this is it, this is it"—the inlaid scales of Justice in the Diwān-i-Khās, Red Fort—Delhi

the last Hindu Emperor of India, Prithvi Rāj, so that his queen might view the river Jamnā every morning from its summit. The great Minār, built in the 13th century, is thought to have been designed by Muslim architects and constructed by Hindu craftsmen. Inscriptions from the Koran are exquisitely carved in the red stone of the Minār. From the Qutb Minār's summit, one commands a view of historical buildings equaled only by that of Rome.

The glories of the seven Delhis are many. But perhaps the most colorful of all, to the sojourner in India, is the lyrically strange and colorful atmosphere which is present-day, everyday India. An evening of relaxation in a garden of poinsettias and palms with the raids of bright green parokeets into the trees of *gul mohar*; the pure melody of Rājpūt women laborers' song as they trudge home from the city dressed in bright red, orange and green flowing skirts, barefoot, but with shoes in hand; and the rare dignity of passing camel caravans—Delhi has its charm, and India, its past and present glories.

Night Tonga

The clatter of the canter
Of a pony over stones,
Reminder of the banter
Of a chatter which intones
Of petty darts of gossip
Like the cracking of a horsewhip
As an emphasis of worship
Of the tongue.

Resounds insistent rhythm
From the distance coming near,
Refracting as a prism
To deceive the listening ear.
Approaching yet receding,
Its resonance is misleading
But the tonga keeps proceeding,
Sound unstrung.

Quick progress of a carriage
Through the night of settling dew,
Whether funeral or marriage
Or a quiet rendezvous,
Coming from mysterious distance
In a waxing-waning sequence
To four beating hooves' insistence
It has sung.

Servants

Yunas Khān, typical head bearer

Abdul Majīd, bearer

The author's bearer and his two children, New Delhi

“WHAT IS INDEED THE NOBLEST TONE AND REACH OF LIFE FOR MEN?”

—*Ruskin*

THE SALUTES and *hazurs*, the salaams and ready agreements of *jī, sāhib*, the jump to attention at my entrance—this behavior of Indian servants never ceased to cause me certain embarrassment. If the intelligent, educated Indians, in efforts to abolish social disabilities of their people, urge the eradication of a “slave-mentality,” it is no less incumbent on all those who are served, and especially on Westerners in India, to rid themselves of a much-too-common “master-mentality.” I marvel at the accomplishment of most of my servants—accomplishment so striking when set up against their relative opportunity. I remain extremely grateful to the good men who served me so well and helped make my life so enjoyable while I was in India. Wherever we were able to work together, and when we came to know one another as people, away from servant-master relationship, we worked happily and effectively.

Categories of servants run the gamut of countless menial tasks. Specialization in these tasks assures wide and frequent employment. I shall speak here only of those servants who kept our bungalow in running order. There were, in all, nine of them.

My colleague and friend, Pat (Maureen Patterson of Ann Arbor, Michigan), and I were in charge of our bungalow, formerly a Rājā’s “palace” in New Delhi. We ran the place for ourselves and three other Americans. The five of us required nine servants to manage comfortable living.

Most closely responsible for my own well-being in India was a young man named Abdul Majīd. He served Pat and me as our personal bearer. Abdul’s duties included serving our meals, getting us up in the mornings, taking care of our clothes, running our errands, dusting our rooms, and seeing to the finer points of housekeeping.

Abdul came to us in the usual way. We were in the market for a bearer. We asked our office servants to send us friends of theirs who would like the job, and we also asked a few of our friends to recommend a bearer.

When applying for a position, the servant brings with him a series of *chits* or letters of recommendation collected through the years from those he has formerly served. We turned down one bearer on the strength of one of his *chits*, which read, "Habib has a distinct distaste for memsahibs." When Abdul turned up, we learned from his *chits* that he had been considered an honest, reliable, and willing bearer. Later, we learned that he had worked for Mohammed Ali Jinnah, the Muslim League leader of India. So Abdul was hired—at Rs. 45 per month (approximately $13.50).

Most of our other servants came to us with the bungalow. They included the *māli* (gardener), *khānsāmān* (cook), *masālchī* (assistant bearer), *dhobi* (laundryman), *chokra* (the young boy who assisted our cook), and *mehtar* (sweeper). Two other bearers took care of the three other people in the house.

The servants with their families lived in the bungalow's servants' quarters. They shared a common compound, two bathrooms (one for women, one for men), and one water tap. They organized their own household tasks on something of the same basis on which they ran our house, i.e., the sweeper cleaned and the *dhobi* washed for the other servants. In these quarters lived 29 persons.

Abdul is a Muslim. His wife, Seliman, observes *pardāh*, the system of seclusion of women common among Muslims. When she visited us, I saw the *burqa* (the covering and veil) for the first time at close quarters. Seliman is a shy and attractive young woman. The *pardāh* system restricts to members of her own family her association with men, and it requires that, whenever she ventures out, she must wear the veiling *burqa*. The *pardāh* system is rapidly breaking down in India. It is unlikely that Abdul's young daughter will carry on the custom. Abdul himself explains that the institution of *pardāh* is an expensive and undesirable one, and he adds that the older members of his own and his wife's families are those who insist upon it.

Abdul has two children: five-year-old Abdul Majīd, Jr. and one-year-old Abdul Wajīd. Children are children wherever you find them. The older boy, whom we called "little Abdul," is a shy lad but, once we had won his confidence, he played ball with us and helped us construct windmills from the Tinker Toys we had given him for Christmas.

Our *masālchī*, Saiyid, daily demonstrated the great potentialities for education among India's servant people. His duties were those of dishwashing, carrying food from the kitchen, and generally assisting the bearers. Saiyid had had no formal education. But, somehow, he had taught himself to read. I could look out from my bedroom and see Saiyid sitting, when he had a spare moment, on the kitchen steps, book in hand. Saiyid was always there when the electrician came, and after a few months with us he could repair our switches. And when our bicycles broke down just before a trip into town, it was always Saiyid we called to repair the part.

It is quite possible to live for years in India without learning more Hindustāni than the rough imperatives of *āo* and *jāo* (*come* and *go*). But, as always, one finds that a knowledge of the language is invaluable in coming to know the people and the culture. Not only is it culturally useful but, with servants who do not readily understand English, a working knowledge of Hindustāni often avoids awkward situations. When Pat and I chose the servants, we chose those who did not speak much English—we were keen on increasing our own knowledge of Hindustāni. Saiyid could read some English, but he did not understand the spoken language well.

One day, Jim, one of the Americans living in the other part of our bungalow, determined to explain to Saiyid that he must wash the glassware in scalding hot water. Not knowing Hindustāni, Jim gesticulated and explained himself in terms of "hot," "very hot," "water," "glasses." Saiyid appeared thoroughly satisfied with the explanation and agreed to carry out the sahib's wishes. Jim retired to his room, pleased with his accomplishment. After a few minutes Saiyid entered, carrying on a plate a glass—and the glass contained "hot," "very hot" water, recently boiling. This on a summer day. Jim resignedly took the glass, thanked Saiyid and resolved that he should pick up a few more words of Hindustāni.

The Hindu *māli* cultivated our extensive gardens. He was at home with our flowers, which ran through many varieties from small carnations to towering poinsettias, and with vegetables from *brinjals* to Jerusalem artichokes. The *māli* was a most charming chap. With all the dignity and grace of his flowering plants, Chiddu Rām moved about the garden and, on special occasions, came to our door to adorn us with garlands and neatly appointed corsages. It seemed almost an impertinence to pay him a meager Rs. 35 per month ($10.50), but this represented a 40 per cent raise over his last salary.

The day the *māli* came down with cholera was both a terrible and an interesting one. Abdul informed us that morning that the *māli* had fallen ill the previous day. One of my Indian friends, a medical student, was visiting us. She took a look at him and then announced that Chiddu Rām probably had cholera. Abdul took him to the hospital. And in the days of his recuperation, it was our good servant, Abdul, who took the *māli's* wife across New Delhi to visit her husband. The interest for us in all of this lay in its further demonstration that Muslims and Hindus do live and work together and befriend one another in the best of neighborly fashion. On the personal level, there is little doubt about essential amity among Indians.

Our household sweeper and his family lived in one of the most centrally located sections of the servants' quarters. As is true with most sweepers, Makān is a so-called Hindu "untouchable." His duties were to clean the floors and the bathrooms, build the fires and do the less agreeable work around the house. He came to me, one day, asking for a *chit*, which would safeguard him when he made the trip to his village with a pair of goats he owned. This was not an unusual request—servants are often stopped by the police and required to prove ownership of anything they may happen to be carrying with them. My *chit* assured him safe passage across the Jamnā bridge and on to his village home.

The *dhobi* and his wife and family of two small boys and an infant son kept an admirable house. Clean and bright, this family seemed to thrive even on the meager allowance Mohammed earned. The *dhobi* is, you know, the washerman. In traditional fashion he beats one's clothes on rocks to assure that they are properly cleaned and, quite incidentally, assures that they are properly riddled. I soon found that, with a box of soap flakes, Mohammed was quite willing to wash out the finer things with less energy.

The *dhobi's* young son set up his own bicycle repair shop with a few odd tools just outside our front gate. He spoke in terms of establishing a real shop and then of handling automobiles, and before we left he was talking even of airplanes.

The servants did live together in surprising harmony. But it was only natural that, living in such crowded quarters and having so little extracurricular activity to consume their time, energy and interest, the servants now and again should have their small quarrels and their petty differences.

One day, Jim came to me with the tale of an altercation between his bearer, Ibrahim, and the *dhobi*. It seems that the quarrel started over a shirt. The *dhobi* had, allegedly, failed to iron the shirt in time for Ibrahim to have it back for the sahib. Pat and

Abdul and the author in a *tangā*, New Delhi

Tufail Ahmed, office bearer

The author with little Abdul and the *dhobi's* daughter

I were called in to interpret and to settle the quarrel. After much discussion with the two servants and with witnesses, we decided that Ibrahim had been at fault. Strangely enough, Ibrahim's brother, Solomon, took the *dhobi's* side. When Ibrahim realized that the decision was against him, he very dramatically announced that he could not bear the situation, and that he would resign and leave the house. Always a temperamental chap, Ibrahim apparently had chosen this as the best face-saving device. Jim agreed that Ibrahim should go, and said he would get another bearer. The following morning, we learned that Ibrahim had turned up to serve breakfast and, when Jim reminded him that he was leaving, Ibrahim, in an even more dramatic manner, had protested. "Leaving, Sahib!?" Following this surprised query, he pointed out that Jim was as a father to him, that he didn't know where he would go nor what do, and, finally, how could Jim do such a thing? The problem was returned to Pat and me for resolving. We called the group together again, and there ensued a most remarkable scene. The *dhobi* made a beautiful speech, the essence of which was that all men are brothers, and if Ibrahim wished to stay on he would be mightily welcome. And after so saying, the *dhobi* embraced Ibrahim. Then Solomon embraced the two of them—and Jim, who was left quite astounded, managed to ask what in the world they all were saying. Ibrahim, who is a Christian, and the *dhobi*, who is a Muslim, resolved their differences in this admirable manner—another demonstration of communal amity in everyday affairs.

We tried to have the servants come to us whenever they were in trouble. Usually, their moments of distress came over financial difficulties. One day, Abdul came to us asking for an advance payment of his salary. We enquired into this sudden request. He, with some embarrassment, explained that the *bania* (moneylender) demanded Rs. 180, then threatened to break up his house and beat him if he did not pay immediately. We learned of the exorbitant rates of interest exacted, and we easily understood how so many Indians are ruined by inherited indebtedness. Abdul's situation was easily resolved. We gave him the full amount and then proceeded to subtract it, month by month, in small amounts from his salary.

My experience with Indian servants has convinced me that dishonesty is, with them, a matter largely of necessity. When we explained to our servants that they should consult us whenever they were in need and on whatever score they wished, we found that they did not resort to dishonest means for solving their problems. In no case did we lose property or money; the servants were thoroughly trustworthy. Abdul always took the money to pay our bills and, on several occasions, we found it necessary to entrust him with over a thousand rupees in cash. This was as much as he made in two years. Yet on no occasion did he take or lose a *pais* of the money. Perhaps the most remarkable of all was the frequent opportunity all the servants had for taking our things. The bearers, the *masālchī*, and the sweeper always had ready access to our rooms. Abdul carried the key to our house for, after all, he had to enter and awaken us every morning.

The procedure of awakening, if it had not happened every day so early in the morning, would have been most entertaining. I was to be awakened daily at 7:15. On the dot of 7:15, Abdul would slip into the bedroom and very softly announce, "*Sawā sāth baje hogaya, missāhib*" (it is 7:15), and then he would set down on the bedside table a tray of fresh papaya or tangerines and a pot of tea. Of course, I promptly went back to sleep. A little later, in a voice slightly less gentle: "*Missāhib, sārhe sāth baje hogaya*" (it is now 7:30)—and faithful Abdul would not go away until I was well up in bed and drinking my tea.

It is of interest to compare the treatment of servants in Indian and in "western" households. If I were an Indian servant, I should prefer working in an Indian household. The pay, in rupees, is usually not so high, but servants of a well-established Indian household are so much a part of the family life that they have a sense of belonging which is, for them, invaluable. The children are cared for, the servants are looked after, and the prestige of the servants is often that of the prestige of the house. The servants take an honest pride in their work; they know that the household is as much theirs as their master's.

To recall our various *khānsāmāns* is to think at once of poetry and American pie. Cooking for Westerners is no mean job in India. We seemed never to be satisfied—and it was largely a matter of American pie with us. I have never seen such art nor such skill in cooking as I have in India. With practically no utensils and nothing more than a charcoal fire built into the stone wall of the kitchen, our cooks turned out most delicate pastries in designs which served as reminders of the artisan skill of those who fashioned the Pearl Mosque. There was nothing wrong with the skill of our cooks. It was simply that we could not put across the idea of American pie. Even the Muslim cook who wrote impressive Urdū poetry could not apply his imagination in that direction. And the last cook we had, in the best of spirit, tried time and time again. But thanks to American pie we lived on a series of most unusual and delicious desserts. These varied from deep dishes covered with delicate pastry to small, cake-like, covered tarts. It became a huge joke—and when we asked the name of some rare dish Abdul served us for dinner, he always grinned broadly and announced, "American pie."

Thanks to the good servants of our New Delhi bungalow, I came first to know the common Indian and his life. And through the hot dry *lu*, the beating sudden rains of the monsoon, and most of all through the strange and often unreasonable demands of our foreign customs, these good people served and helped us.

I shall not forget, Abdul, the many nights you disturbed your sleep and neglected your own comforts to dash onto our roof-terrace and rescue us from a monsoon downpour—nor the bitterly cold nights in our unheated rooms, when you brought your own little charcoal burner and your own meager ration of charcoal to cheer and warm us while, had we allowed it, you would have returned to shiver in your own colder quarters—nor the trips you made to the bazaars through blistering midday heat, even during the Ramzān days when you, true to your religious faith, were taking neither food nor drink from sunrise to sunset, so that we might have ice to cool the drinks, which you then served with a smile in spite of your own parched throat. I shall not forget you, Abdul, nor our artist *māli*, the alert Saiyid, nor the neighborly *dhobi*, the faithful sweeper, nor the good-spirited *khānsāmān*. I continue to wish you well—you and the whole of your good Hindustān. And you have inspired me with a faith which results in a great deal more than benevolent well-wishing.

Thatched Are the Roofs

Thatched are the roofs of wealthy men
And mud the walls which house them when
From fields at dusk they come to rest,
But know not what they have possessed
Of riches rarely manifest.

Companions of the friendly cow,
These wise men of a timeless now
Commune with soil and sky and cloud,
And care not they remain unbowed
To gods or men or binding crowd.

There where the bullock made his round
And by his labor sweetness ground,
The cane lies cut upon the hill
To feed again the good gur mill
And wealthy men with fields to till.

Thatched are the roofs and mud the walls
And grander than the gilded halls
Of kings, the well-robed and the great
Who learn to worship and to hate
Their gods, their crowds, their cursed fate.

Udaipur, the Heart of Rajputana

Setting out for an excursion by camel, the author and Maureen (Pat) Patterson at the edge of Fateh Sāgar, Udaipur

"...The gorgeous East showers on her sons barbaric pearls and gold"

Mewār, cradle of the mighty Rājpūts, pivots around the ancient state and city of Udaipur. One of the 562 native Indian states, Udaipur is the realm of His Highness Mahārājādhirāj Mahārānā Shrī Sir Bhupālsinghjī Bahādur, in point of blueblood, premier in the whole of India.

To speak of Udaipur is to speak of enchantment. Before setting out for Rājpūtānā, I had heard that Udaipur is the Switzerland and the Venice of the Orient. But my estimate of Udaipur is something quite apart from stereotyped forms of beauty. Udaipur is unique. Here are crater-forming hills and tropical isles back-dropped by gleaming forts and other trappings of the Medievalists. Here are palaces and palms and all the shadings of charm. And yet the thing which sets Udaipur apart is not so much its elements of beauty, but rather the delicately weighted pattern, the balance, the design into which these elements are fitted. Udaipur bears much fondling.

The Udaipur design takes its center weightage from the great palaces; palaces and noblesse make up a broad motto theme. The old palace, built on the heights of the city as proper palaces are, commands an authoritative view of the miles of city and jungle and hills which stretch out and away from it. The old palace, with its fine mosaics, gold and gilded inlay, thrones and jewels guarded by stalwart Rājpūts, is essentially the parent palace and the most imposing thing in this walled city. Rising from the very edge of the water of Lake Pichola, the old, white, marbled palace is set off by octagonal towers and the cupolas so characteristic of Rājpūt architecture. The courtyard of the palace extends towards the east where, at the extreme end, the state elephants are stabled.

Other palaces, delicate structures, are settled into the clear water of Lake Pichola. The greatest of the lake-palaces is Jagniwās. Built for beauty and for refuge from the heat of Rājpūt summer days, the palace is of many tiles inlaid in cool walls. Here successive *mahārānās* have tried their skill at decoration and invention. The great swimming maze, a marble lotus flower with water separations, poses the problem to handmaiden swimmers of how swiftest to reach the center throne of black marble to claim the garland and the praise of the ruling prince. Here is the mirror-topped table, useful to noble necks when nobility would view the ceiling murals. And Jagniwās boasts the great mirror walls opposing a stage on which court dancers indulge their art. The mirrors are used by lesser nobles who, with turned backs, follow the dancing performance and are again reminded that they, being less noble, are fit only to gaze upon reflected glory.

The Mahārānā's bedroom suite in Jagniwās is lined 'round with murals. The door and forward walls are adorned by the "beautiful and famous ladies of India"; another wall presents a lake-bird-sky mural; and a third, the life-size portrait of His Highness. The leather-seated, carved, and tiled bathroom of Jagniwās is one of the few bows Udaipur makes to the 20th century.

Through the carved frames of windows in Jagniwās, one may catch the view of another of the lake palaces, Jagmandir. Like some kaleidoscopic miniature, the royal palms and orange groves of Jagmandir show up in almost overly realistic, three-dimensional clarity. As one approaches Jagmandir by launch, the carved white marble elephants seem to reach out and down into Pichola's water. The throne of marble, the fine archways and, finally, the mosaic inside the central cupola were designed by the Emperor Shāh Jahān, who later built the Tāj Mahal. On this noble island are princely orange groves, and papaya trees that bear the most delicious of royal papaya fruit. The lake palaces are befitting. And the princely touch is everywhere.

Marble throne on Jagmandir, lake-palace, Udaipur

The great Old Palaces of Udaipur with the author, Pat, and Abdul in boat

The lakes and the hills and the jungle growth save Udaipur from becoming overweighted by the palace theme. A trek by elephant up to the mountain fortress of Sajjangarh reminds the visitor that the tiger's realm lies close in. The assault of white, long-tailed monkeys on a visit to the royal cenotaphs, and the evening feeding of hundreds of deer fresh from their jungles, assures one that civilization has not utterly encroached.

As guests of the State, my companion and I benefited by the raw feudalism which is Udaipur. We ordered quiet riding camels "for ladies" and took a turn around Fateh Sāgar, another of the great Udaipur lakes. We viewed the remarkable slave girls' garden, Saheliyon-ki-Badi, considered one of the most beautiful gardens in the whole of India. Here is demonstrated another great feat of ancient Indian engineering. The pressure of water brought down from the reservoir of Fateh Sāgar causes delicately cast silver birds to whirl about ejecting interweaving streams.

The largest temple in Udaipur, known as Jagdish, is built to the god, Vishnu. The engraving, originally worked in 1651 A.D., is remarkably distinct. The plinth of the temple is of unusual height, requiring thirty-two steps to mount.

Udaipur's bazaars boast the great handicraft centers of woodworking, silversmithy, and dyeing and printing of cloth. The hardy Rājputs, resplendent in fuschia turbans, and Mewāri women, gay and buoyant in multicolored *sārīs*, buy and sell and carry on their business even as it has been carried on for the many centuries of Mewāri history.

A walk around Lake Pichola in the face of the setting sun is something incomparably enchanting. The women of the city go down to Pichola with brass *lotās* neatly balanced on erect heads. The infrequent Muslims of the community pray towards the setting sun. A party of mourners sets up its ungodly wail in remembrance of one deceased. And occasional Mewāris describe

Feeding monkeys at royal cenotaphs, Udaipur—
Maureen (Pat) Patterson and the author

The author mounting elephant for trek to Sajjangarh, Udaipur

their way of life in terms of ancient Rājpūt proverbs, whose points generally escaped me.

The palaces and the jungles, the jewels and the sepia-colored hills—themes of anachronistic civilization set against splendor of natural topography—are finally brought together in one of the most remarkable developments in the whole of the Udaipur scene. This is the event which takes place every evening at sunset at the place known as Khās-Odi. An event terribly natural and yet, in concept, terribly artificial, the feeding of the wild boars at Khās-Odi is something which could happen only in the heart of Rājpūtānā. To view this climactic scene, one mounts a fortress-like building and walks out onto its marble balcony. A man appears with a basket of grain and ventures out into the craggy slate-like arena below us, just off the jungle. He shouts wildly a distortion of the Hindi word, "*āo*," which means "come." Soon, we hear pigeons fluttering into the place. A few peacocks make their appearance. At last, a wild boar comes poking out of the brush, and then another and another. Rather suddenly, the scene changes, and beasts and birds come charging and beating their way from the jungle. They go nosing about for the scattered grain—first a few, then a dozen, and now hundreds of them. Off they start in a circular movement. The man continues his shouting—more wild boars, more peacocks, and more pigeons. The stamping of feet amid the crunching and clattering of broken slate, the flapping of wings, the foolish chattering of pigeons and the screaming of peacocks are punctuated by more and more frequent shrieks from the wild boars. Here is a frenzied, primordial excitement. As dust clouds rise higher, the intensity of bestial greed mounts; the mad medieval inferno is complete.

Udaipur is medieval feudalism and, to the visitor who gives it but this superficial glance, there is in Udaipur the charm and beauty and enchantment such as can be found in this 20th century only in the odder corners of the world.

Udaipur Spring

The season once again swings round:
Birds nesting,
Blossoms unfulfilled
Tell hopeful tales.

Of winter wasted
Let another sing,
Denying spring.

Prerogatives are for the young
While we the wise
Search, sedulous,
A season's spirit.

Sing then another song:
Of torture-laden spring.
Make tenderness the tragedy.

But to this single sentiment
Give pause because
Such tenderness the brave become:

With spring begun
The winter's done.

Modes of Dress

The author and an Indian friend wearing *sārīs*

The author in Panjābi *pājāmā* and *qamīz* with *chūnī*

The author and Pat wearing *pājāmās*

“Weavers, weaving at break of day, why do you weave a garment so gay?”

—Sarojini Naidu

The keynote of dress in India is informality. And through dress alone one often can learn much of the background, regional home, religion, and occupation of the wearer. The variety in dress is so great that one can easily move about the streets of India's cities dressed in almost any costume without drawing undue attention.

For the women of India, the most common mode of dress is the *sārī*. Adjudged the most beautiful garment among all garments worn by women the world over, the *sārī's* graceful lines and the soft fall of its pleats provide an easy artistry, which is unmatched. Consisting simply of six yards of straight cloth, the *sārī* has manifold advantages. There is never a problem of fitting and styling; any *sārī* will fit, and become, anyone. The problems of keeping or packing are reduced to the barest minimum. Hats or any other form of separate headgear are ruled out by the use of the end of the *sārī*, known as the *pallā*, which may be brought up over the head.

The secret of wearing the *sārī* is in its “wrapping”—the term used to indicate the donning of the garment. To complete the dress, one must have a well-fitting blouse. The *sārī* is tucked into a floor-length petticoat, wound around the waist once, pleated some six or seven times, wrapped once more around the waist, and brought up over the left shoulder. There are slight variations in the manner of pleating and arranging the *pallā*, which is usually thrown over the left shoulder to hang down the back.

Sārīs run the gamut of texture and pattern, from the coarse white cotton piece to the finely spun “shot” Benārsī *sārī*. Dress *sārīs* usually carry elaborate borders, often heavy with real gold or silver thread. *Sārī* borders vary according to current fashions.

Comparable to the *sārī*, the *dhoti* is worn by a majority of Indian men. Like the *sārī*, the *dhoti* is simply a straight piece of material varying from four to six yards in length. It is wrapped to form a loose-fitting trouser-like garment. But unlike the *sārī*, the *dhoti* is relatively unattractive. Nonetheless, those who wear the *dhoti* proclaim its many advantages of comfort.

Colorful and distinctive, the many turbans of India fill the streets with interest. From the neatly wrapped low-tilted turban common to the region of Mewār, to the high-crowned turban of the frontier Pathāns, the turban marks the man. There is the majenta-red of Rājpūtānā, and the popular pale blue turban of the northern Sikh. Turbans drying in the sun may stretch their twelve yards from tree to tree, and turbans knotted on coolies' heads may soften towering loads of luggage.

But when we have spoken of *sārīs* and *dhotis* and turbans, we have just made a beginning. Of all the other modes of dress, we must speak first of the *pājāmā* and *qamīz*—for this is the dress of large sections of people, especially the Muslim and Sikh men and women of the Panjāb. The *pājāmā* is a baggy garment; the close-fitting *qamīz*, a long shirt worn over the *pājāmā* to some three or four inches above the knee. This costume for evening wear may be of the finest silk and handiwork. When worn by women, the costume requires a *chūnī* or *dobatta*—a scarf thrown in varying fashion over the *qamīz* and around the shoulders or over the head.

Muslim men frequently wear bright fezzes. While it may be assumed that all men wearing the fez are Muslims, it is not true that turbans are worn exclusively by Hindus or Sikhs. My bearer, Abdul, a Muslim, sported a variety of headgear. Ordinarily, he wore his dark red fez with black tassel. But he also boasted a Frontier fur cap and, for serving company tea, he wore his freshly starched, firmly wrapped white turban. There are, too, the special headgear of other communities, such as the small, black, mitre-like cap so distinctive of the Pārsī community.

We owe many of our words of dress to India. *Pājāmā* is one. *Jodhpur* is another. The tight-fitting riding breeches which we know as jodhpurs is the customary male attire in the princely State of Jodhpur. Known as *tang pājāmā*, the breeches are covered to below the knee by an *achkan* or *shirwānī*, a type of tight-fitting coat especially becoming to slender men.

The shoes of a well-dressed Indian may be the up-turned, pointed, gold *jūtī* or, perhaps, hand-embroidered slippers. Like so much of the Indian dress, the shoes are designed for sheer beauty. The custom of frequent removal of the shoes assures Indians remarkably healthy feet. I like to recall the facility with which Indians use their toes. The skilled workers make good use of these added digits. I have often seen carpenters sawing wood, holding the piece between their feet and sawing down a very narrow margin between toes. And not only are workmen skilled in this way. One of my good Indian friends reached out with her toes and picked up a fragile figurine from a small table in our living room. My friend, Pat, expressed considerable alarm lest she drop it, whereupon my Indian friend replied, "You must remember that these are Indian, not American, toes."

Variety in dress is notable, but ornament is equally varied. The small red or black dot worn on the forehead by young Indian women, especially Hindus, is variously known as *bindi* or *kum-kum*. It is applied with powder or liquid, or pressed on in the form of a thin celluloid disk. *Alaktak*, or *alta*, is a red liquid applied to the soles of the feet. The Indian counterpart of our mascara is *surmā*. But the Indian *surmā*, properly used, succeeds in setting off the true beauty of the eyes. Earrings, bangles for wrists and ankles, rings for fingers and toes, and nose ornaments are often worn.

Costume in India is rarely a problem. I have appeared on the streets of India's Imperial Capital dressed in Western clothes, in *sārīs* of varying make and color, in slacks, in *pājāmā* and *qamīz*. I have, in each case, felt quite comfortable. I have not yet disappeared into the privacy of a Muslim *burqa*, the veiled and robed outer garment used by women observing *pardāh*—but as to the social comfort of the *burqa* there is, again, little room for doubt.

Kadhi (cotton)

Now the Kadhi took its form
Powerfully, finely woven,
As I waited a thread was richly born
Idly and madly was spun.
As I watched it, another, delicately shaped
Faintly but surely touched me
Among others the while it was finely draped
Entwining, enhancing the first.

I thrilled as weaving it faster and faster
That noble design was thus woven.
The strands—first one—but now a million
Not for themselves—now no longer threads
But parts of that thing—of that art—
That thrilling, powerful masterpiece
Which stirs spirits though long since dead
Into life with self soon to cease—
To cease living for merely self
But to be a part of something great
Like those tiny strands in the Khadi
Parts of the whole which challenge fate.

Agra, City of the Taj Mahal

The author at the Tāj Mahal

"THY CHANGING KINGS AND KINGDOMS PASS AWAY,
THE GORGEOUS LEGENDS OF A BYGONE DAY,
BUT THOU DOST STILL IMMUTABLY REMAIN"

—*Sarojini Naidu*

THE 125 MILES stretching between India's Imperial Capital, New Delhi, and the City of the Tāj Mahal is best traveled in the days following the rains. The lush growth of grasses and grains—interrupted by tall clumps of palm trees, animated by wild peacocks and antelope, and backdropped by a setting of biblical-looking women at biblical-looking wells and rustic goat-herds in command of India's oddly beautiful spotted goats—fills up distances between ruins of ancient tombs and monuments. Mathurā, with her walls teeming-full of monkeys, is the only city stop in these 125 miles. And beyond Mathurā, along the curving course of the sacred River Jamnā, lies Agrā, made famous by her Tāj Mahal and again beautiful by her monuments of other ancient greats.

If one is to do the usual thing, one approaches the Tāj Mahal by *tangā*, the popular horse-drawn, two-wheeled carriage of Northern India. From the center of the city, one must find his way through bazaars and puddles, around bullock carts and camels, to the great bridge spanning the Jamnā. And there, standing with its back to the sacred river, facing out onto one of the most beautiful gardens in the world, is this great white jewel which we know as the Tāj Mahal.

It has become the fashion among certain circles of persons, who would variously term themselves critics or skeptics, to express disappointment upon the first and then successive viewings of the Tāj. But as I passed through the adorned main gate, salaamed by the Khādims, and stood full aface of the great tomb,

I knew why people come the world over to gaze and exclaim, and I knew why long-time residents of Āgra could not miss seeing the Tāj at least once a month by the light of a full moon.

The beauty of gardens of tropical verdure and flowering color begins at the very edge of the expansive grounds that provide the setting for the great Mahal. The natural beauty continues over 42 acres until, inside the massive red sandstone gateway, it finally surrenders itself to the artful beauty of the Tāj's splendid architecture.

The main gateway to the Tāj is too often neglected in favor of the mausoleum itself. But the remarkable carving on the gateway's marble arch, an inscription from the Koran done in blackstone, is some of the finest carved Arabic calligraphy in the world. Artisans have traced in such excellent perspective the Tughra inscriptions inviting the pure to enter the garden of paradise that the letters appear to be of the same thickness at the level of the eye as they appear at the top, a distance of 80 feet from the ground. The mosaic on the arches is of colored stone, and four minarets set off the four corners of the gateway giving precedence to 22 small domes, 11 of which crown each of the archways on the inner and outer sides of the gateway structure.

The reflecting pools with five single-jet fountains mirror the Tāj Mahal and extend the length (850 feet) between the outer, main gateway and the basement of the great tomb itself. The walk down this length points up the immense size of the Tāj—for it had seemed to loom so close to the outer gateway—and yet it is not the size of the Tāj Mahal which is most impressive.

The grand mausoleum stands on a double platform. The first marble platform is four and a half feet above the ground. In the center, the second platform, 313 feet square, rises 18 feet above the first. The higher marble platform is paved with alternate squares of black and white marble. At its four corners are the minarets rising to a height of 162½ feet from the surface of the

The author with two Indian friends in the garden of the Tāj Mahal

Looking from an opposing cupola towards the main gate of Itmad-ud-daula

The author and Chandru at Itmad-ud-daula

garden. The mausoleum proper is in the center of this platform measuring 186 feet square with a central archway 66½ feet high at each of the four sides.

After mounting the steps to the first level of the monument proper, one is required to put on special over-shoe slippers since, of course, the Tāj Mahal is a building sacred to Muslims and must not be desecrated by the touch of shoes. Climbing a few more steps, one enters onto the main porchway at the foot of the minarets. One of the Khādims, descendent from the original keepers of the building employed by the Emperor Shāh Jahān, who built the Tāj Mahal, is entrusted with guiding visitors through these revered passageways.

The incredible carving of the marble grillwork, like fine lace, greets one at every turn. The inner walls are bright with all manner of inlaid semiprecious and precious stones. Inlaid in marble, the cornelion, turquoise, jasper, ajuba, onyx, lapis lazuli, malachite, topaz and many other stones, brought in the 17th century from all parts of the East, trace patterns in the delicate shapes of flowers and the angular beauties of geometric design.

The tombs of Shāh Jahān and Mumtāz Mahal, his queen, lie under the Cenotaph Chamber, surrounded by the lattice-worked octagonal marble screen; the chamber is richly carpeted and illuminated. The enclosure is so finely ornamented that 61 tiny pieces of precious stones make up one small rose. Everything appears in mosaic and inlay. The bodies of the Emperor and his queen lie in tombs directly below the Cenotaph Chamber. On the tomb of Mumtāz Mahal, the 99 Muslim names of God are inscribed in bold relief. The inscription on the Emperor's tomb, translated, reads:

> "The illuminated sepulchre and sacred resting place of His Most Exalted Majesty, dignified as Razwan, having his abode in paradise and his dwelling in the starry

heaven, dweller in the regions of bliss, the second lord of constellation, Shāh Jahān, the king valiant; may his mausoleum ever flourish, and may his abode be in the heavens. He travelled from this transitory world to the world of eternity on the night of the 28th of the month of Rajab 1076 A.H. (1666 A.D.)"

A flashlight would be a comforting accessory for climbing the minarets of the Tāj Mahal. The passageway up 164 winding steps is as dark as a starless night. Along the whole of the ascent, there are only two tiny windows which allow small slivers of light. But emerging onto the summit of a Tāj minaret takes one away and across the city of Āgra, across the River Jamnā and back to the magnificently polished dome of the Tāj itself with its gilt pinnacle rising to a height of 270 feet from the level of the river. The heat and the wind atop the minaret on an Indian August day is incredible—but so is the Tāj and the whole of the city of Āgra.

The romance of the Tāj Mahal should be experienced in many of its facets. To view the Tāj at midday is yet another thing from viewing it at sunset or again at sunrise. The Tāj in moonlight, submitting its white surface to the embrace of a full moon's rays, is of such special character that the moment of viewing almost escapes full conception.

Each time I viewed the Tāj Mahal, I went away marvelling. Once away, I knew somehow that there must be something wrong with this architectural wonder. It usually occurred to me that that something was to be found in the dome. Each time I returned to the Tāj, I looked more critically. Perhaps it's true that the balance of dome and minaret is faulty. But perhaps the Tāj is disturbing because we cannot yet accept such close approach to aesthetic perfection.

The city of Āgra has its Tāj Mahal and, in contrast, it also has its portion of India's miserable masses. Not unusual anywhere in

India, and so hardly surprising in the environs of the Tāj Mahal, is the sight of a father carrying to the burning *ghāts* a small, white bundle that contains the dead body of his infant son or daughter. And as famine strikes this great land, the little bundles increase, and the people consider themselves fortunate if they have the cloth in which to wrap the dead or, indeed, if they have the energy to burn their dead. There is misery in India—a misery made great by the selfishness of men, and a misery for which India is scarcely responsible. The great *mahals* (palaces) and the beauty of Indian handicraft continue to bear mute witness to the potentialities of India's people. And so, through *mahallās* (slum areas) and the alleys of hovels, one should, when in Āgra, make one's way to the remarkable mausoleum of Mirzā Ghiyas-ud-Din Beg known as Itmad-ud-daula.

Itmad-ud-daula is my favorite among the lot of Āgra's splendid monuments. Its beauty is less awful than the Tāj Mahal's; its delicacy, more humble. The screen surrounding Itmad-ud-daula's cenotaphs is of the most finely spun marble lace in this city of incredibly fine craftsmanship. Her mosaics and inlaid work are of the loftiest design and execution. Itmad-ud-daula, even more than the Tāj Mahal, can well afford to scorn those who would describe her. Her beauty is of such refinement that words alongside her are as presumptuous as they are inadequate.

One can scarcely leave Āgra without a look at the mammoth fort. And a look would entail an entire afternoon's worth of amazed observation. Both Hindu and Muslim architecture mark the variety of structures within its walls. The imperial balcony of white marble inlaid with mosaic flowers of jewels; royal bathtubs where emperor and wives bathed in rose water supplied by scores of servants from an underground marble platform; the Pearl Mosque as beautiful as that of Delhi; the black slate throne; the Saman Burj (octagon tower) aglitter with jasper, agate and bloodstone, and topped with golden domes; and, finally, the tiny

South face of Rādhāswāmī temple under construction at Dayāl Bāgh

A marble cutter at work at Dayāl Bāgh

stone set in just the proper place to catch the reflection of the Tāj Mahal across the sacred river—this was the native place of emperors.

To skip over the great works of the Moghuls at Fatehpur Sikrī and Sikandra in favor of setting down a few notes on the current construction at Dayāl Bāgh may seem to have neglected undeniable artistry for an architectural work of doubtful value. But the Rādhāswāmī temple now in process of construction at Dayal Bagh provides an important interest, if one of a different sort.

Some two miles from Āgra lies a complete little community within the limits of the village of Dayāl Bāgh. Inhabited entirely by members of the new Hindu sect known as "Light of the World," the Dayāl Bāgh community is erecting a monument which they hope may rival the ancient mausoleums of northern India. Meanwhile, the community works towards the propagation of their belief in Rādhāswāmī, its founder, and the major tenet that the highest good comes from serving its own community and administering to the needs of its members. The Dayāl Bāgh monument has been under construction for fifteen years. Plans provide for its completion in another forty.

The main part of the building is now complete, and much of the inlay and carving has already been executed. Here one may watch workmen going about their work in much the same way as similar men did similar work in the days during which the Tāj Mahal was constructed. One may watch a pair of men sitting at a block of marble with a primitive saw consisting solely of a strip of metal with a wooden handle on one end and a stone weight on the other, dipping a mixture of gravel and water onto the surface of the marble and pulling this crude saw back and forth, the gravel serving slowly to cut through the huge slabs. They told me it takes fifteen days to cut through a small column. This is a country which knows the value of patience.

In the Āgra bazaars—the author and friend Pat

The inlay work of the mausoleum is, in places, beautiful, but in others, even now, almost too ornate to achieve the loftier elements of beauty. In an effort to indicate the unity of mankind, the designers of the Dayāl Bāgh monument have worked into the building a variety of scripture in a variety of scripts. Sanskrit writings, beautifully executed, are inlaid in varicolored marble; nearby, Arabic script is used; and around the edges of floral designs, Roman letters, carved and inlaid, indicate the botanical names of the represented flowers.

Climbing stairs to the second story, one may look down into the crypt which houses the tomb and the ashes of Rādhāswāmījī, founder of the sect. Gold and many-colored marbles are worked together in oriental ostentation. It is unlikely that this mausoleum will rival the beauty of the ancient works—but the variety and ornate design of Dayāl Bāgh, after the intended forty years, may well defy the imagination for sheer elaborateness.

It is difficult to leave the city of the Tāj Mahal, the place of Itmad-ud-daula, and the many scattered gems of architectonic grandeur. Yet Āgra lives on in all her tradition and one has only to return—even in memoir—to touch again her greatness.

Love Lost

Where, beloved, do the stars speak, sevenfold,
Your soul's delight?
Where sings the harmony
Which spins your finite sphere?
Speak, beloved, where?

Lie you along some pearl-caked pond
Or wander, lost, among the pines,
Or now perchance sit you amidst
The salty seeds of crystalizing tears?
And search the shadows' symmetry
For substance such as you and I alone
Can understand?

Oh, yes, beloved, here to me
The shadow of your soul has fled
Where wanders now the thin and slighted shade of mine
—Yet, can you know?

For where are you, beloved—
Where are you and what?
The long, the lengthening, the last, last mystery.

Animals in India

The author on the lawn, New Delhi,
with bullock in foreground

"THE COW IS A POEM OF PITY."

—M. K. Gāndhī

WHAT of lions and leopards, snakecharmers and sacred cows? The thought of India, homeland for one out of every five persons of the world, has somehow always conjured up in our minds frequent pictures of the stalking tiger and the wiles of snakes. And yet, I was in India for some weeks before I saw a snakecharmer.

The most elementary use of discriminative thought will point up certain facts about the much-vaunted animals of India. India does boast of jungles full of wild life. The extensive growths of Assam or the Central States may produce subhuman life to satisfy the most difficult of animal lovers. But the streets of Delhi and Bombay can do little more for him than turn up stray dogs, cows, goats and, if he is a foreigner, an occasional snakecharmer-magician, who may also produce a performing bear from some Himālayan reaches.

In spite of my bearer, who insisted that the deserted village in the vicinity of Chirāgh Delhi was deserted because of ravaging *sher* (lions), there is very little likelihood that, with the best of *shikār*, one could encounter in India an honest-to-goodness real-life lion. The species is all but extinct in India, and estimates of the number of lions extant in the whole of the country (these are found mostly in the Forest of Gīr in Kāthiāwār) run in the lower hundreds. But if you would have tigers, that is quite a different matter.

The famous tiger-shoots of India continue unabated by war or Hinduism. Tiger-shooting remains the great sport of Westerners in India and of occasional Indians who have the position, wealth, and irreligion to undertake it. Many a Hindu is appalled by the great *shikārs*, their intention and their progress. And after one's first impressed reactions to the color and fanfare of the *shikār*, all this pomp and circumstance and, indeed, the lack of sportsmanship in shooting tigers in the traditional fashion may well appall not only those who hold respect for all life, but those alike who would regard a relative human dignity.

The best locale for more impressive tiger hunting is one of the princely states. In Jaipur, I learned from the Rājpūt Colonel, who leads the *Shikār-Khānā* or Hunting Department of the Jaipur government, something of behind-the-scenes management of tiger-shooting. This gentleman is responsible for producing tigers in the proper place at the proper time to be shot at by the princely retinue or the guests of the State.

The Colonel explained that, several days before a scheduled *shikār*, he sends out a party of beaters into the sections of the Jaipur jungles where he believes one of "his boys" (tigers) can be found. The beaters, setting up an impressive clamor, drive the beasts in the direction of the shooting-box. The several shooting-boxes, established on heights in proper jungle settings, are fitted with the comforts common to awaiting, and then shooting, animals which cross the line of vision. Here the "hunters" rest and watch. On the appointed day the *Shikār-Khānā* will have arranged for one or several tigers to cross in front of the shooting-box. My Rājpūt Colonel assured me that, once he and his men have produced one of their "boys" and sent him across that spot, their responsibility has been fulfilled. If the Mahārājā or his guests do not then bag the tiger, that is not the department's fault.

Of course, tigers are occasionally hunted and shot from elephants, but the shooting-box is the favorite. An approved method of producing the tiger in the proper place involves the tying of a live cow or buffalo in the clearing near the shooting-box. After the beaters drive the tiger near this spot, the scent of fresh meat takes the beast on. He makes the kill, gorges himself and proceeds to take his rest after a full meal in the nearest thicket. The timing requires a thorough-going knowledge of tiger-lore, for the *Shikār-Khānā* cannot have the tiger asleep when the Mahārājā wishes to have a shot at him. But this is the department's business, and the Colonel has an excellent record—he always produces tigers.

An important function, of course, of the hunting and shooting department is that of protecting the State from man-eaters. A healthy, active tiger will, I have learned, be quite free from addiction to man-eating. It is only when the beast becomes lame or old, so that he cannot stalk and win other game, that he will lower himself to man-killing and man-eating. The Jaipur Colonel explained that the reason for tying a buffalo in the clearing and not a man (he was, I think, being facetious) involves this understanding of man-eaters. But man-eaters must be stalked and destroyed. In answer to my question, the Colonel said that beaters are occasionally killed. In fact, the business of tiger-shooting is a very bloody affair.

Tiger-hunting, or as it is more properly called in India, shooting, has its sister-sport of "pig-sticking." This involves considerable courage and activity on the part of the "sticker." It can more properly be termed "sport" than can tiger-shooting. Wild boars are the game—and they can put up a most determined and ugly stand. This *shikār* involves skilled horsemanship. The boar may be pursued for miles through open country before he is overtaken. The "sticking" is accomplished by a spear thrust into the boar, preferably between his shoulders, just behind the head.

The use of animals to add to the pomp of stately circumstance is no better illustrated than at a *darbār* or a princely celebration of some holiday or special occasion. The ruling princes vie with one another in increasing the number of elephants maintained by their respective States. In gold and brocade and

Boarding the Mahārājā's elephant at Jaipur

Camels and small white mosque on the outskirts of Delhi

jewels, these beasts are paraded in festive processions and made to carry, in immense howdahs, equally ornamented noblemen. Elephants may be had by State guests at any time for treks through jungles or to mountain fortresses. In some places, elephants are attached to temples. It was in Ceylon that I learned temple elephants can be quite haughty, and that the greater of them are best left undisturbed.

The elephant is a delicate animal. I didn't really accept this, although I had heard it, until I took my first real elephant trek to the Sajjangarh fort in Udaipur. I had seen elephants bathing in rivers, I knew that they are not to be worked for more than four hours a day, and I also knew that an elephant's grooming includes a full pedicure. But on my trek to Sajjangarh I was to learn that it is unwise to keep an elephant waiting; I had kept my elephant waiting at least a full hour.

The trek was to take several hours. My friend, Pat, and our bearer and I met the two *mahāwats* and our elephant about five o'clock in the afternoon. We were, as I say, an hour late. The path to the top of the young mountain was somehow especially tortuous—at least the experience of those of us in the howdah interpreted it as tortuous. The wringing motion of an elephant is something which I hadn't quite bargained for, especially since I had only recently been abed with jaundice. And I soon learned that an elephant cannot be hurried.

When we arrived at the fort on the summit, the sun had long since set, and the *mahāwats* seemed a bit anxious to start the descent immediately. In spite of my well-wrung side, I realized that I was no one to argue with two *mahāwats* and an elephant. We started down the increasingly tortuous path as the full moon rose. The jungle overgrowth on either side discouraged me from doing my own walking back to Udaipur.

Abdul, in his red fez with black tassel, looked much dismayed. The elephant was in very bad temper. With *mahāwats* shouting and urging him on with sharp-pointed prods, we progressed down towards the valley. The elephant, poor fellow (for we had kept him waiting), behaved as though he might at any moment launch his own non-cooperation movement. He gave warning by spraying us periodically with his trunk. The *mahāwats*, the moon, the red fez and black tassel, the jungles, and the temper of an elephant kept waiting marked that Udaipur trek. We made it on towards the distant lights of Udaipur and, when we reached them, I knew a great deal more about the delicacy of elephants.

Of all the animals I know, the camel feigns the greatest dignity. The supercilious and smug attitude of this cud-chewer never varies from his moments of participation in the caravan to his awful awkwardness of kneeling to take on a rider. An old Indian saying explains the camel's haughtiness: "Man knows 99 names for God, and the camel knows the hundredth."

Elephants and camels are important animals of state—but they have their more practical uses, too. In parts of India, elephants are used for construction power, and camels are employed as drayage animals throughout the whole of northern India.

From the lowliest roach to matter-of-fact lizards, there are some Indian animals which will insist upon living with you. After the rains, insect life, even in semi-arid Delhi, flourishes. One finds that leaves of the *nīm* tree discourage the more forward of such creatures as would riddle one's clothes. And one early learns that lizards simply must be tolerated.

My friend, Pat, and I had some seven or eight lizards living with us. The two largest ones (about eight inches in length) lived in our bathroom. Ordinarily, our lizards were well-behaved. Our bathroom lizards kept to their quarters, comprised of walls and ceiling, when we were anywhere in sight. As much could not be said for one young lizard who lived in our bedroom. Poor Pat was to discover this one July afternoon as she lay on the *chārpaī* trying to sleep out the heat of the day. Her shrieks brought me

Baby elephant, Ceylon

running, only to find that our wayward lizard had found his way up under her blouse. In the ensuing fracas, the issue was settled by the lizard, who left his tail behind and managed to depart in much confusion. He sulked until he grew another tail and then decided that blouses and beds were strictly extra-curricular.

There were occasional other times when my experience with animals in India seemed to illustrate the crossed purposes of man and beast. I had felt a kindred sympathy with the slate-grey crows which sat about Delhi in the summer with beaks hanging open, pantingly, but mutely, complaining that the Indian sun was unrelentingly unmerciful. But after a summer of sympathy there came, on one December morning, an experience of disillusionment with the slate-grey birds.

Winter in Delhi is as uncomfortable, in the other direction, as is summer. Very little provision is made for heating buildings. So it happened that we conceived the bright idea of eating breakfast in the garden to take full benefit of the ever-present sunshine. On this December morning I was complimenting myself upon having moved outside and was enjoying my usual breakfast. I had just picked up a piece of buttery toast and was carrying it to my mouth when the beating of wings, a slate-grey vibration in my face, and a rude plucking at my hand shocked me into the realization that I had been divested of my beautiful piece of toast. The servants were called and, while Abdul served the rest of the breakfast, several alerted servants with poles and shouting attempted to give us protection. But the second time, poor Abdul was the victim. Out from the kitchen he came, carrying a platter of eggs and sizzling bacon. He did very well, really—managed to save the platter and lost only one piece of bacon. The eggs were a bit ruffled, and things had to be reconstructed before we could carry on. I should add that the whole company of us retreated indoors. The slate-grey crows continued to enjoy the ever-present sunshine, and we shivered daily over breakfast in our dining room.

It is a complex subject, but I cannot talk of animals in India without mention of the cow. Since it has frequently been asked me, I have stopped chuckling over the amusing query of "which cows in India are sacred?" This is, of course, a matter of perspective. There is nothing about a cow which would mark it as being intrinsically sacred or not sacred. The quality of sacredness is always an endowed quality. The question, properly stated, should rather be, "To whom in India are cows sacred?"

This is relatively simple. The cow is sacred to all who believe in the sacredness of Life. This is basically a concept of orthodox Hinduism.

There is much misconception in the West about "sacred cows." The cow is, for the average Indian, the epitome of all subhuman life. The cow, then, represents all animals. The cow stands in a premier position among animals in India for many reasons economic in basis. It was by the products of the cow that the ancient Indians lived. Milk and milk products are still of primary importance in Indian life. For these reasons, the cow is looked upon as an animal of primary value.

To describe one tenet of Hinduism in terms of the "sacredness of the cow" is an oversimplification of the broad and profound doctrine of *ahimsā* (non-injury). Mahātma Gāndhī once said, "The cow is a poem of pity." This is a poetic expression which partakes of essential Hindu attitude.

The cows, unmolested as they walk the streets of an Indian city, mean a great deal more than we usually accredit them. That great numbers of these animals are underfed is not surprising. The reason lies more basically with the economic problem of India. The problem of the cow in India is economic, not philosophic.

Cows continue to produce much of the life-food for Indians. There are great dairy farms in parts of India, and there are repeated projects for raising their productivity.

Sacred cows and snakecharmers—why is it that we in the West have concentrated so much of our thought of India around them? Snakecharmers appear and behave very much as one expects them to behave. They may be hired to give a performance of their charming. The good ones come with two large saffron-colored bags full of cobras. They sit on the ground, free the snakes, and, piping in the pure melody of Indian tunes, sway slightly before the snakes. The cobras are charmed—by the movement, not the music. I am told that cobras are deaf.

Outside of the saffron-bagged cobras, I saw only one snake during my stay in India. That one happened to be a baby cobra. We found him in our dining room. I was duly alarmed, even after the infant was safely captured and placed in a jar. When I telephoned one of my good Indian friends with the query, "What do you do for cobras?" I received this placid reply: "Feed them bowls of milk." After I had further explained that my primary interest was not to do something "for" the creature, but rather to safeguard the household in case its parents might be roaming about, my friend suggested that I send my bearer out for snakecharmers. I promptly assigned Abdul the task. He went reluctantly. In the evening, he returned—without snakecharmers. He explained that snakecharmers were very hard to find, that they live in the jungles, and that they simply were not to be had in the city. I rang up my friend for further instructions. She was amused. "Did you really send him for snakecharmers?" she asked me. And then she explained that, had Abdul discovered a charmer, the fellow doubtlessly would have brought his full retinue of snakes and, after having distributed them throughout the house, would have proceeded to collect them again, following which performance he would have collected a neat fee and left us where we were in the beginning. More practical jokes—but ignorance is patently a vice.

Bullocks drawing water near Delhi

Monkey on Delhi tombstone

The patient bullocks with their cargoes of cauliflowers plod resignedly into Delhi during the night hours. The rainbowed peacocks grace the countryside or, if run afoul of hunting man, may please the palates of those who relish cold peafowl served with chutney. Impudent monkeys hurl stones from rooftops and gather coconuts from palm trees. The wild jackals scream from the tombs of India's monumented dead.

The animals of India serve and harass and amuse humanity in their own Hindustan, and 'round the world they are subjected by antipodal humans to much discussion, as though their importance outweighs that of a fifth of humanity—that fifth which resides, like them, in Hindustān.

King Cobra

Your liquid length elusively
Spills coil on coil of creeping flesh
Your tail and scale and belly thresh
Amid the dust seductively.

Your diamond-studded kingly skin,
So moist, so bright, so keenly taut,
Displays a shadowed style inwrought,
Suggests a wily discipline.

Your flattened face and cool-teared eye,
Your brittle jaws which house within
The forked tongue, symbolic sin,
Potential wickedness belie.

When stretched and straightened coil from coil
Know that despite majestic hood
You cannot stand as kings have stood,
Return to slippery sullen toil.

Ajmer and Pushkar,
King of Sacred Sites

Busy street scene in Ajmer

"One man calls on Rāma, on Khudā another, one implores Gosāyan, to Allāh others pray—"

"There is nothing in Ajmer but a mass of ruins, just like the rest of India." This was the estimate of an Italian woman who was returning after some years to Ajmer. That she had added "just like the rest of India" gave me good reason to expect much from this Rājpūt center. A ten-hour layover in Ajmer before continuing the journey into Rājpūtānā was to justify my faith in "a mass of ruins."

Settled down into the natural setting of monadnoks and hog-backed hills, Ajmer was enhanced in its beauty by the good Rājā Ānājī, who, in his day, constructed the eight mile Ānā Sāgar, the city's beautiful artificial lake. The famous Shāh Jahān (of the Tāj Mahal) constructed marble pavilions along Ānā Sāgar's embankments. And to the back of the pavilioned lake lie gardens of orchids and roses.

In spite of Rājās and Emperors, Ajmer derives its greatest fame from a saint. The famous Khwāja Muinuddin Chishti, Muslim saint of the early 13th century, lies entombed in the center of the city. And to Chishti's tomb, from all parts of India, come both Muslims and Hindus to honor the memory of this great man, great among the many great saints of Ajmer. Again, the famous Dargāh Khwāja Sāhib, as the tomb is popularly known, was described to me in terms of "filth" and "squatting people." But when I visited that place and looked beyond the courtyard with its "filth" and into the groups of "squatting people," I recognized the Ajmer Dargāh as a place of true significance. For beyond the marble lattices and beyond the enormous cauldrons from which, on special feast days, the people of Ajmer and Merwāra come to "loot the *deg*," I saw the tomb of Chishti. And at the tomb of Chishti, both Muslims with their bright fezzes and Hindus in turban and *sārī* worship and revere together the memory of a great personality. Therein lies Ajmer's true greatness.

The magnificent Arhai-dīn-ka-Jhonpra mosque at the edge of the city of Ajmer is one of the best examples of combined Hindu and Muslim architecture in the whole of India. The screen fronting the mosque is carved with consummate skill, the craftsmanship likened to that of the great Qutb Mīnār at Delhi.

The adjoining ball of the mosque with its 70 pillars, each carved with intricate figures and geometric designs, displays the splendor and artistry of Hindu craftsmanship. No two pillars are alike, not even the two central opposing pillars, where the Hindu architects have come closest to making a bow to symmetry; two-thirds of the way up the columns, the figures are placed at variance with those opposing.

In Ajmer, I visited my first Jain temple. In the heart of the city, the temple, Nasiyan, displays a courtyard ornamented with a tower set off by marble elephants. This temple of the Jains, and especially the temple's museum-like back rooms, is strange to behold. After climbing many stairs, one looks down from small balconies into mammoth and high-ceilinged theaters replete with gilt representations of Jain mythology. Nasiyan confounded even my taste for things rococo. Gods piloting flying elephants and peacocks suspended from glass-bobble ceiling mosaics, hundreds of pairs and braces and couples of lions, tigers, horses, bullocks and other animals, armored warriors and naked youths, palaces, towers, 13 circles separated by glassy water, miniature continents—I could hardly refrain from commenting that, after all, perhaps the creation of the world was such confusion (shades of its progress) and, at the same time, I fondly recalled the carnival merry-go-round and Woolworth's at Christmas time.

Ajmer is a Rājpūt city, and the bazaars and by-paths are, as ever, fascinating. But ten hours is limiting, and the "King of Sacred Sites" in the whole of India—Pushkar—lay only seven miles away.

We drove the seven miles in a well-mellowed Citröen. The drive through the foothills was, again, one graced by peafowl and camels and colored by wild ring-tailed monkeys, white against red sandstone.

Pushkar is built around the sacred lake. And down to the lake's edge, Hindu pilgrims come to bathe in the healing water. I arrived in Pushkar just before dusk. The last rays of the sun struck out onto the sacred lake, rimming the monadnoks in the background and illuminating the gentle people as they came down to the *ghāts*. And back into the village of Pushkar towered the temple of Brahmā, the most famous of the rare temples to Brahmā in the whole of India.

Perhaps the most remarkable temple in Pushkar is the temple to Vishnu, Sri Rangjī, built by Madrāsi Brahmans in all the splendor of south Indian architecture. The neatly executed rococo carving of animals and birds proves immeasurably pleasing to those who appreciate ornament in architecture. The temple is flanked by grounds kept incredibly clean. In the back, the garden shelters sacred peacocks and blossoms in remarkable flowers of many colors. Structures built around the temple house Brahmans and their families. The atmosphere is one of dignity and grace. But here, for the first and only time during my stay in India, I saw frank discrimination against the "untouchables" or "scheduled castes." A sign at the entrance of the temple courtyard reads: "Untouchables are not permitted in the temple grounds."

A view from atop the temple of Brahmā and the quiet atmosphere of Pushkar at sundown provided a foretaste of the charm of Rājpūtānā. Ten hours were not enough, but Udaipur lay ahead of us.

Recognition

The moon is full and frightened are the ghosts
Who range the bleaker corners of the tomb
To search along the fringes all the coasts
For sweeter, silent, sympathetic gloom.

With untried step another probes the haunt—
To hunt the ghosts—and, startled, seeks to feel
The warmth of living flesh he used to vaunt,
The life he could from death so ill-conceal.

For one the other in its time became:
The fearsome and the frightened are the same.

Food and Famine

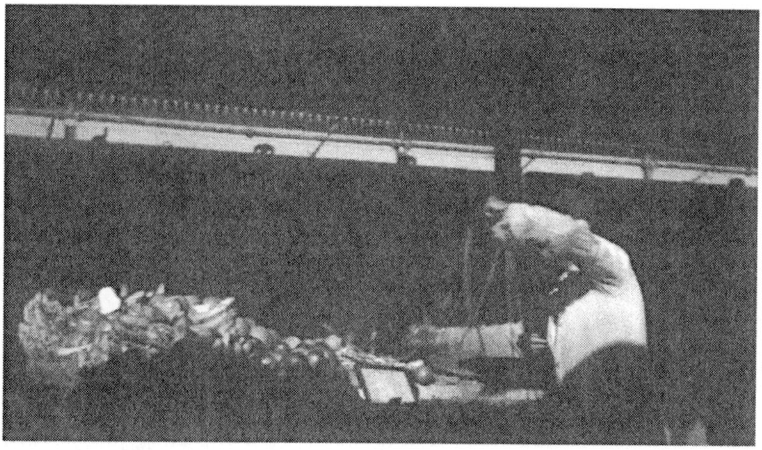

Fruit *wallah* at Delhi railroad station

"By food the living live..."

—Bhagavad Gītā

FAMINE in India is both actual and impending. I have been urged to note down some of the food customs of which I learned during my stay in India. But I cannot speak of food and India without first commenting upon the critical consideration of famine. More seriously than ever before in her history, India is threatened by tragic lack of foodstuffs.

Famine on such a scale as was experienced in 1943 in Bengal is a product of our own age. When reckoning the toll of war, we must not fail to count the Bengal man-created famine casualties, variously estimated from one million and a half to three million dead, and countless millions crippled by malnutrition. If we are to assume our fair share of responsibility in a world which would be One—a responsibility which mounts high when tallied against our own bounteous resources—we must not forget that now, in 1946 and on into 1947, at least ten millions in India lie under the dire threat of even greater, more terrible famine.

The relish of a chicken curry or a mango chutney is one of many fond memories of India; the accusing stare of a starving child is one of the fewer, but manifestly lasting, impressions. If I am to speak here of the curries and chutneys, I must also give reminder that much of India is starving.

Like so many things Indian, the food of India is a subject vast enough for volumes. The variety of culture and of custom provides a wealth of dishes with almost infinite variety in seasoning, mixture, preparation, and presentation. I can hope to note here only a few of the dishes which I enjoyed in Indian homes and to indicate broadly some of the food customs which I experienced in northern India.

A majority of Indians are vegetarians. Vegetarianism is a tradition based on the Hindu conception of the sacredness of all life. Most orthodox Hindus find it repugnant both to belief and taste to kill for the sake of eating. But one must not make the mistake of assuming that all Hindus are vegetarians. Large sections of Hindus do eat meat, some partake only of fish, and yet others will not eat eggs inasmuch as eggs contain the elements of life. Orthodox Muslims, on the other hand, will not take pork, although they do eat other meats. And orthodox Sikhs will eat only the meat of animals which are killed with a single stroke. These religious customs are widely observed in India. Nonetheless, it is quite possible to sit down at a table of Indians of all religious communities and partake of a meal with them. At a dinner party I gave shortly before leaving India, there were twenty-one Indian guests. Among these were several Hindu vegetarians, several Hindu non-vegetarians, a Sikh, a Muslim vegetarian, a Muslim non-vegetarian, to say nothing of several representatives of other religious communities. We ate dinner together and shared a thoroughly enjoyable evening without thought that we had cut across many religious and communal frontiers.

Of primary importance in the Indian diet are both wheat and rice. Wheat is the chief ingredient of the *chapātī*, a tortilla-like, unleavened cake that takes the place of bread in the Indian diet. Rice is used as a base for curries, of which there are a seemingly endless variety.

An Indian dinner, which may be eaten with the fingers from plantain leaves while sitting on the floor, or which may be eaten from a table with western table utensils, centers around the curry or the curries. The curry dish is cooked in a curry sauce made from any variety of spices and their combinations. Typical of such dishes are: chicken curry, vegetable curry, mutton curry and the like, with the main ingredient, other than the curry, indicated by the specified type. The rice, either boiled or fried, is served first. It is properly taken out onto the plate (or plantain leaf), and then covered with the curry. Several types of curry may be served at the same meal.

Dāl, a type of pulse, is an essential food in the vegetarian's diet. It provides protein, and may be served in a variety of ways. A delicious dish, the most usual form of *dāl* is the boiled *dāl* pea, resulting in a rich yellow color and eaten along with curries and/or *chapātīs* in the main meal.

Chutney is, of course, popularly used to dress up the Indian dinner. Variety, again, is the keynote. All the way from the spasm of infernally hot chutney made mostly from chilies to the pleasure of a sweet mango chutney, this relish may take on characteristics running the gamut of subtlety in taste.

Indian food is frequently, for the Westerner, too spicy, too "hot" for daily consumption. I shall never forget the many times I fell victim to the common practical joke of feeding the unsuspecting (even after many months) foreigner a *pakorā* or a *samosā* assertedly "new and sweetly delicious," and then, in fact, offering a disguised green chili. The joker is quite safe, for his victim is thereby utterly immobilized. There follows what could most accurately be described as a "cooling off period" before relations are reopened.

Very popularly used are curds made into any number of dishes and served frequently in place of dessert. *Dahī*, an unsweetened dish of this type, is most commonly used and may be eaten with the main part of the meal. *Shrikhand* is a dish of sweetened curds, and *rabadi* combines both sweet and sour curds. They are often served topped with pistacchio nuts and decorated with refined silver or gold paper, which may also be eaten and is reputedly beneficial to the blood.

Other common sweets are *jalebis* made from flour and fried in batter; *rasagulas* (this is a favorite in Bengal) made of flour and curds; pistacchio *vādā*, a type of candy akin to our brittles.

For hot weather refreshment, there is nothing like the Indian *sharbat* and the strange *palūdā*. *Sharbat* (from which our word sherbet is derived) is an Indian fruit punch. It may be made of mangoes or any of the many types of melon common in India. It should contain much of the pulp of the fruit. *Palūdā* is like nothing I have ever before experienced. Served in a cup or small bowl, *palūdā* is made of the grain product our nearest approach to which is vermicelli. Pieces of this Indian vermicelli, cooked and cooled, are covered with a sweetened syrup seasoned with some fruit flavor and mixed with cracked ice.

My favorite Indian recipes are too numerous to give here. I have chosen a few of the more typical favorites, which I have set down here as they were given me by an Indian friend.

Indian Recipes

Ālu-ke-kofte (potato balls)

Ingredients: Four or five potatoes; one slice of bread; salt; fat sufficient for deep frying.

Method: Boil the potatoes. Peel and mash them thoroughly, so that they can be made into smooth balls the size of large walnuts. Add salt to taste. Soak one slice of bread in cold water for about ten minutes. Squeeze out every drop of water from the slice of bread, and then add it to the mashed potatoes. Mix thoroughly. Make small balls and drop them into hot fat (deep as for frying fritters). Fry until golden brown in color. Serve hot.

Spinach *Pakorās*

Ingredients: Graham flour; chili powder (optional); salt; spinach; fat for frying.

Method: Mix flour, salt and chili powder in a bowl. Make a hole in the center and add water, very little at a time, gradually working in and mixing the flour with water to make a very smooth batter the consistency of cream. Wash the spinach leaves thoroughly and coat each leaf separately with the batter. Fry in deep fat. The fire should not be slow. Test the temperature of the fat by dropping in a little of the batter which, when the fat is properly heated for cooking *pakorās*, should rise *immediately* to the surface.

Cauliflower Pickle

Ingredients: One cauliflower; one-half bottle vinegar; one teaspoon salt; one-fourth teaspoon chili powder.

Method: Cut the cauliflower into small "flowers." Sprinkle salt and chili powder on these pieces. Put into an airtight jar and pour vinegar over the cauliflower. After two or three days the pickles will be ready for use.

Mutton Chops

Ingredients: Mutton chops; salt; vinegar; pepper; cardamom; cinnamon.

Method: Boil mutton chops in salt and one to two tablespoons of vinegar with just enough water to make them tender. Heat one to two tablespoons of fat. Lightly fry them in a flat frying pan, sprinkling the powdered ingredients on top. Cover the chops and cook them for 15 to 20 minutes on a very slow fire.

Samosās

Ingredients: Potatoes; peas; salt; chilies; flour; fat for deep frying.

Method: (1) Prepare the filling: Boil the peas and potatoes and crush them with a fork. Heat one-half tablespoon of fat. Mix the crushed ingredients with salt and chilies and heat for a few minutes in the fat. (2) Covering: Mix flour with water to make a stiff dough. Take a little bit of the dough, make it into a small ball half the size of a walnut, and with a rolling pin roll it out, round in shape, sprinkling a little dry flour on it now and again if necessary. (3) Cut the circle in half. Place the filling in the center of each half. Trace the outline of the semicircular half with the finger dipped in cold water. Fold one end of the half over the filling and the other end over that. Press the double edge down to hold the filling. The final shape of the *samosā* is that of a wedge (as a piece of pie). (4) Frying: the fire should be moderate, and at no time very hot. Fry in deep fat as one would make fritters.

The Living Strive

A last full drop hangs on the pitcher's lip,
Awaits the round of time, insensible,
Fulfills a sterile parting, forced to slip
To nothingness, the ineluctable.

The insensate sphere clings fast to dipping rim,
Unmindful of the jug-womb's emptiness,
His own reluctance creature of time's whim
And he himself unfelt and meaningless.

A-dangle from glazed lip the poised ball
Presents from time his petty comedy.
Yet were the jug, the drop, the parting fall
Of human stuff, it were a tragedy.

The living strive to intercede with time
Destroying both the rhythm and the rhyme.

Rishikesh on the Sacred Ganges

Main street in Rishikesh

“Fair and tall as holy hermits
stand yon shadow-mantled hills,
murmuring mantras with the zephyr
robed in threads of sparkling rills...”

—*Rāmāyana*

Down and over the lower slopes of the Himālayas, *Gangā Mātā*, Mother Ganges, discovers her way into the plains of India. And at the place where the great river greets those plains stands the city of Hardwār. Up from Hardwār, along the snaky river course, faithful Hindus make their pilgrimage; the hardy and enduring pilgrims may hope to follow *Gangā Mātā* to her very source. Along their pilgrim's progress, they stop and rest and worship at successive villages, which provide them shelter and haven until they recapture the strength and courage to move on. Such a village is Rishikesh.

Together with an Indian friend, I made my own pilgrimage to Rishikesh in the latter midsummer days of 1945. Chandru and I set out by train for the Himālayan hills with little more preparation than an eagerness to experience the fresh relief of the hill country. We took a few provisions: tinned foods, water purifier, and a few medicines. My bearer, Abdul, went with us. In the spirit of things, we took no time-piece. We were ready to lose ourselves in the younger reaches of the Ganges.

From Hardwār, we traveled by narrow gauge rail through forests of vegetation ranging the hillsides from the exotic to the ridiculous—the white beauty of the deadly belladonna, and the odd trees shooting in ascetic deviation straight to the skies before affording themselves the luxury of foliage. Among its hills and into a Ganges bend snuggles the village of Rishikesh. Through the mud of a recent rain, we sank our way along the village paths and sought a place to stay.

Rishikesh boasts many *āshrams* and *dharmsālās*, charitable inns for pilgrim wayfarers. We stopped at one of these shelters to ask if we might stay. The *sādhu* in charge of the hostel, in friendly but doubtful manner, replied that we were welcome to stay, but quickly added that we likely would find the accommodation very uncomfortable. He urged us to seek a more convenient place. We continued into Rishikesh. Another *āshram*, maintained by the people of Sind, seemed a likely place. We entered the courtyard, removed our shoes and went in to talk with the keepers of this hostel. They welcomed us, but added that we surely would find the place inconvenient—we could doubtlessly find a more comfortable shelter.

As we made the rounds of *āshrams* in Rishikesh, I became aware that, somehow, I was quite out of context. The replies we received at each *āshram* were sincere in the welcome—but somehow the misgiving was that "the European" would not find the place to her liking. People of my ilk were, after all, hardly expected to penetrate this part of India. There was no foreign accommodation.

We were tired and discouraged. At last, Chandru suggested we call on a *sādhu* who was in some way beholden to her father—he would surely take us in. We mounted the stone steps to his Sikh *dharmsālā*. Chandru enquired of saffron-robed holy men if she might speak with her father's friend. Unfortunately, the *sādhu* had gone to Haidarābād. Nonetheless, the saffron-robed ones offered us a hearty welcome, but explained that we would find the accommodation most inconvenient. We assured them we were well prepared for inconvenience, and that we really should like to stay. Their welcome had, indeed, been genuine.

When we walked into our quarters—two barren, stone rooms with nothing but several *chārpaī* for sleeping and a hole in the wall for cooking—I grasped the truth of what we had so frequently been told: the accommodation was, without doubt, inconvenient.

Chandru chuckled. "This will do you good. I daresay you have never lived in a place like this before."

She was quite right—on both scores.

After the initial shock, I began to catch the charm of the *dharmsālā*. We looked out over the very narrow, crooked street which led immediately down to the Ganges. Our windows were nothing more than openings in the building fitted with a few iron vertical bars. The bars, I soon realized, served the useful purpose of keeping out monkeys, who plied their traditional mischief as best they could in spite of bars. Our privacy was, at every point, intruded upon by the stares and chatter of these fellow primates. Anything left close to the window ledge was fair game for monkey hands.

We opened out our sleeping bags, and then realized that we were fairly starved. As soon as Abdul had been sent forth in search of food, I summed up our situation. It then struck me that, if I were to interpret things in the manner usual with foreigners in India, I should consider the situation quite remarkable. "Do you realize," I asked Chandru, "that this is very odd? Here we are—you a Hindu, Abdul a Muslim, and I something of a barbarian from 'across the black waters,' and we all are staying here in the heart of the land sacred to Hindus in a Sikh *dharmsālā*."

"And why not?" she rejoined me. And, indeed, why not?

Part of our inconvenience was a matter of bathroom facilities. We finally struck on the bright idea of bathing at the railway station. This was something of a trek, at least three-quarters of a mile. The stationmaster, to our surprise, greeted us and easily agreed to unlock the bathroom twice daily for us. His extreme cooperation was explained when he addressed my friend as "doctor." Chandru was, in fact, still a medical student—but somehow the word had spread through the village that she was a doctor. When she explained, he remained friendly, congratulated her on having undertaken such a worthy and needed profession, and continued to supply us the key to the station bathroom.

For the first days of our stay in Rishikesh, we consumed most of our time in fulfilling bare necessities. Our twice-daily trek to the bathroom, our struggle to find food and prepare it, and our tiffs with the monkey population proved a day's work almost in themselves.

Every evening we heard the chants and the music and the prayers of the *Gurdwārā*, the temple of the Sikhs, in the *dharmsālā* just opposite our rooms. One morning, one of the *sādhus* stopped Chandru as she came up the steps. "Tell me," he said, "why do you allow your Muslim servant to cook your food?"

Chandru hesitated for a moment, and then posed this question to him: "Do we all have the same God?"

This holy man with the smile of wisdom replied, "Young woman, you are wise—do what you like so long as you are here."

Abdul was somewhat conspicuous with his little red fez among this Hindu population. But he made friends and moved about with seeming pleasure through the bazaars and in the village.

In reviewing our food problems, we decided one day that we must somewhere procure eggs. We had become, through necessity, vegetarian. But, in Rishikesh, not even eggs could be had. Abdul agreed to make the trip to Hardwār to get eggs. When he returned late that evening, he told us his tale of egg procurement. It seems that he had been stopped by the police and questioned about the U.S. army musette bag that we had let him take along. I shuddered to think of poor Abdul languishing in a Hardwār jail. But Abdul had had a bright idea—he explained that U.S. were the initials of his *missāhib*, and it was for her that he had gone for eggs. It so happens that Chandru's surname is Uttam Singh; the

U.S. was a convenient coincidence. He escaped the police and, after some difficulty, procured three dozen eggs from a military cantonment by explaining that he was buying them for an army officer—this, too, on the strength of the "Uttam Singh" khaki musette bag.

Whenever we visited the bazaars—which was often, since we lived on bazaar foods—we enjoyed the satisfaction of mingling with those whose lives had been lived in the remoteness and the pertinence of Rishikesh. We became fond of one gentle fruitseller who greeted us daily with a beaming *namaste* and pressed new varieties of mangoes or pomegranates on us. We termed him the *yogī* of the bazaar—for the man, without doubt, had discovered the secret of happiness and purpose in life.

Visiting the bazaars had its elements of beauty and interest, and even of danger. I never failed to discover something new, something delightful, or at least something remarkable. And I proceeded to remark and to exclaim. Chandru put up with what she considered my "tourist" approach to bazaar scenes for some time. But one day, she found an end to her patience.

"For goodness' sake, Joan," she said to me, "when will you cease to be a raw American?"

I was duly abashed, but I could hardly refrain from justifying my reaction when I recalled the remark two Rishikesh women had passed just the day before. Chandru and I were making our bazaar visit. These two were eyeing us in great curiosity. As we passed them, they made a comment which, in translation and in essence, was this:

"Look at those two—who do you suppose they are?"

"Well, I just don't know. One of them is an Indian, but the other one—well—I really don't know, but you do see specimens like that in Bombay."

The danger of Rishikesh bazaars is tied up with the raucous mischief-making of many monkeys. Monkeys took a special delight in racing along the rooftops of low-constructed bazaar huts. When they were not dashing down into the shops, stealing grain or fruit, they amused themselves by throwing things. As we made our way around cows and people in the main bazaar street, the usual monkeys were up to their usual antics. But one day, the monkeys in question happened to have come across a most threatening piece of iron pipe. It must have taken the largest among them, but he did it—threw the pipe with all his might directly onto us. It was fortunate we were not walking faster. The pipe fell only a short distance ahead, much to the dismay, I think, of our rooftop friends.

We were never free from this monkey business. The first day I walked back with a lovely papaya in my musette bag, I learned the value of camouflage. When I arrived at the verandah of the bungalow, I took out this luscious fruit, and a menacing bull monkey challenged me. "Shall I give it to him?" I asked Chandru.

"Do as you like," she advised, "but if I were holding that papaya, I think I should not quarrel with this chap."

I decided it was all a matter of bluff, but my decision was short-lived. I bluffed as long as I could in the face of a better bluffer whose teeth, I think, were uglier and whose growl was ruder. I bought him off with my beautiful papaya and made quite sure on succeeding days to get well within the house before extracting fruit. We did continue to bring fruit in spite of the retinue that trailed us from the gate, and members who even knocked demandingly on the door.

One day we discovered in the village a *dāk* bungalow—a place neatly furnished for visiting government officials. After some dickering, we managed to move into this bungalow. It was beautifully situated with an extensive yard fronting directly on the river. Inasmuch as the *dāk* bungalow was a much more "convenient" place, we had the time we needed to make excursions up along the Ganges and into the forested hills of Rishikesh.

Bathing steps, Holy Ganges, Rishikesh

Street scene in Rishikesh

The Ganges is young at Rishikesh. Her waters cut roughly through boulders and around hard-capped hills. And up from her banks into Himālayan forests, one finds the natural sanctuary of overhung evergreens and the delight of red-berried shrubs neighboring the miniature lilies.

Hanging onto the hillsides above the Ganges runs the road of pilgrimage from Rishikesh to Lakshman Jhūlā. My first glimpse of that ribboned road was at sunset, as my friend and I cooked our supper on the banks of *Gangā Mātā*. I looked across the right bank and saw my first band of pilgrims: determined Hindus dwarfed by an accompanying plodding elephant. And I smiled as I noted a tiny donkey, his back piled high with bundles, bringing up the rear.

The road to Lakshman Jhūlā is alive with happy, determined, and friendly people. On the banks of the Ganges, many small temples gleam in the light and cast their images in the welcoming river. As a billion drops of Ganges' water make their inexorable way to the Bay of Bengal, giving place to another billion which follow with such tumult in these younger reaches and, in their swift turn, throw the temple's image to succeeding drops, the mirrored, enduring temple reminds the Hindu pilgrim of ancient scriptures and seems to repeat:

> "Birthless and deathless and changeless
> remaineth the spirit forever."

The six miles from Rishikesh to Lakshman Jhūlā is marked by the rich landscape and the beauties of small, white temples. The hearty shouts and singing of pilgrims, as they make their way towards headwaters, brighten the morning with sounds of "*Gangā Mātā ki jai!*"—Hail, Mother Ganges! And, as if by predestined contrast, the leprous beggars lining the first few miles of the road call out for alms. They know, too, that the pilgrim's road is a profitable road.

Bridge across the Ganges
at Lakshman Jhūlā

Temple at Lakshman Jhūlā

Sādhus and *yogīs* and *brahmachārīs* and *swāmīs*—holy men and women—dwell in great numbers in Rishikesh and the upper Ganges country. Many of them have built huts along the river banks and there sit meditating, practicing their holy rites. They may attend the river's many temples, or pipe long hours on reed flutes in the enchanting progression of pure Indian melody.

Before our fortnight at Rishikesh was out, we were yet again to change residence. After we received official word that we were not allowed to stay in the *dāk* bungalow, we cast about for yet another roof under which we might shelter. We were not ready to leave these enchanted hills. Chandru, in a moment of inspiration, sent word to the village "fathers" that we sought some place to stay. The response was remarkable. The good people of Rishikesh seemed determined that we should be made comfortable. A gentleman offered us the use of his empty house near the *dāk* bungalow, and yet another family loaned us furniture. We took up residence in this enormous, white building and lived mostly on the verandah, which overhung the river. There we slept under the stars and, for a few nights, under the full moon of northern India blazing across the Rishikesh hills. We lived on mangoes and *pakorās* and *chapātīs*, which Abdul made on the borrowed charcoal burner. We looked down over *Gangā Mātā* swirling directly below us. In the evenings, we went down to her banks and, sitting only a little apart, watched evening prayers. We heard the sound of the conch shell calling the faithful to worship, felt the calm of white cows at the stream's edge, and followed the fog clouds dissipating in ecstasy the fiery rays of a setting sun, scattering them over the feet of the Himālayas.

The spirit of Rishikesh is essentially the spirit of India. There is dignity and reverence, quietude and thought, recognition of things beyond the hills, beyond the Himālayas—and beyond. There is a subtle knowledge in Rishikesh that life is a unity. There is an atmosphere which would blend the things of nature and of man and of all creatures. There is the elusive rhythm of temple gongs and the call of the conch, the suggestion of elusive bliss and the challenge to lay hold on it. Rishikesh cradles that spirit and waves it on into the plains of India—the spirit, and mighty *Gangā Mātā*.

Song of the Ganges

Out from the lower flanking hills
Swift as the mighty spirit fills
Onto the plains the substance spills
Gangā Mātā, Hail! Hail!

Laugh with the strong eternal young
Flow to a gracious glory sung
Known from the One source early sprung
Gangā Mātā, Hail! Hail!

Down from the heights of earth and Mind
Into the plains of humankind
Come to the sea, refresh the blind
Gangā Mātā, Hail! Hail!

Dhobis washing clothes in *Gangā Mātā*

Epilogue

INNUMERABLE lives are affected by war. Joan V. Bondurant is one of those whose course of life took a dramatic and dangerous turn after Pearl Harbor.

Her work as Research Analyst in the OSS in New Delhi cultivated in her an enduring love of both India and its people. Furthermore, she returned to the United States with a persistent desire to master the concept of non-violence, which she had witnessed firsthand during India's struggle for independence.

To achieve this goal, she undertook a course of study at the University of California, Berkeley, where in 1952 she was awarded her Ph.D. She remained at Berkeley, becoming a Professor and undertaking the work of teaching, lecturing, researching and advising doctoral students in Political Science.

In 1970, she left her post at Berkeley to accept assignment at the University of the Pacific, where she worked in a similar capacity for three years. While there, she received a grant to compile Gandhi's periodical, *Harijan*, and wrote the Introduction to that nineteen-volume series.

In the course of her career, Dr. Bondurant made several additional trips to India. During those trips, she managed to meet with Gandhi, Nehru, Shastri, Gaffar Khan, and all the political leaders of India at the time.

Dr. Bondurant traveled all over India to satisfy her objectives, even putting her life in danger to do so. For example, she sought out the head of the Indian Communist Party and traveled alone through extremely dangerous areas to complete her interview with him.

Upon learning of the work of Khan Abdul Gaffar Khan, a Muslim and close associate of Gandhi's, Joan Bondurant set out on a long and tedious journey to the Northwest Frontier of India to interview this great Commander. He had transformed his army of fierce soldiers into a highly effective, weaponless force. Gandhi referred to such work as the "non-violence of the brave." High in a mountain forest along a rocky road, Bondurant met Khan, and there she deepened her knowledge of alternatives to traditional war-like strategies.

Joan's long trips and travels throughout India were not without a price. She actually lost her health in India. While at a ceremony, a honey-like mixture was passed to her and, not wanting to offend, she sipped it. Shortly after, she was taken seriously ill, and there ensued many treatments and major surgery, leaving her with low adrenal function.

Today, she resides in Tucson, Arizona with her friend and colleague, Edna Cardish, Ph.D.

Although Joan is now legally blind, it is not unusual to hear her tapping away at her typewriter in the middle of the night as she strives, still, to communicate Gandhi's philosophy.

Her publications are too numerous to list here. However, her classic work is *Conquest of Violence*, a book that is still in print after almost fifty years. A revised paperback edition with a new Epilogue was issued in 1987 by Princeton University Press. Dr. Bondurant also wrote the Introduction to Louis Fischer's 1950 biography, *The Life of Mahatma Gandhi*, Easton Press.

Dr. Joan V. Bondurant's initial passion for serving her country through the OSS during World War II evolved over the years into a desire to save the world from perpetual war. She saw, in Gandhi's rescue of India from British rule without any military action, a model for the 21st Century.

May her dream come true!

Edna Cardish, Editor

A Word of Thanks

Sincere gratitude is extended to those women who contributed to the Revised Edition of *Sketches of India*.

Special thanks go to the following:

Ashley Old
Katy Wykoff
Mary Witkowski
Carol Moore
Jean Nelson
Kim Levingston
Marilyn Zellner

This book was produced through the efficient and excellent work of its publisher, Leila Joiner.